Bismillah Little Leyla

WRITTEN BY QURA ABID & ILLUSTRATED BY MONA ISMAIL

PROLANCE

www.prolancewriting.com
California, USA
©2017 Qura Abid
Illustrations ©2017 Mona Ismail

All rights reserved. No part of the publication may be reproduced in any form without prior permission from the publisher.

ISBN: 978-0-615-92178-5

In the Name of Allah, the Most Gracious, the Most Merciful

This book is dedicated to my loving and supportive family, my encouraging husband, sisters and brother, and of course, my little munchkin. I would not have had the courage to pursue this dream without any of you.

Most importantly, I thank God for blessing me with this opportunity to share a tiny morsel of His beautiful religion with all the little mumineen.

The sun comes up and Leyla smiles.
Time to wake up and start the day.

So first what must she say? Leyla knows! Do you? It's

BISMILLAH!

She runs to mommy and daddy and says salaam. Then time for breakfast yum yum yum.

Daddy made pancakes and Leyla can't wait! But mommy says, "First what must we say?" Leyla knows! Do you? It's

BISMILLAH!

After breakfast they head to the park. Leyla goes to wear her jacket, the one with gold stars. But first what must she say? Leyla knows! Do you? It's

BISMILLAH!

Then into the car, but before they go far, first what must everyone say? Leyla knows! Do you? It's

BISMILLAH!

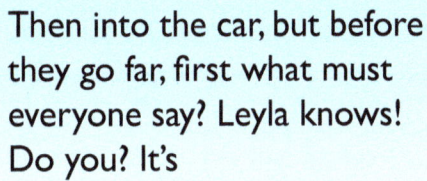

At the park Leyla sees the swings. She loves them! They make her feel like she has wings. Before she gets on, first what must she say? Leyla knows! Do you? It's

BISMILLAH!

Then mommy asks, "Would you like to play soccer?"

Leyla loves soccer and this game is so fun. The ball comes to her and then she runs.

She's about to kick, but first what must she say? Leyla knows! Do you? It's

Bismillah!

Mommy and daddy are so proud! Little Leyla knows so much now. Leyla knows we start everything with BISMILLAH to show that we know Allah is watching and waiting to help. Leyla knows and we should know too.

Say BISMILLAH and Allah will always help YOU!

About the Author:
I am a second generation Muslim-American, born and raised in Atlanta, Georgia, and a mother of an incredible, energetic toddler. I have had a passion for reading from a young age. When I had my own daughter I wanted to share both literature and Deen with her. So, I set out to share with her in my own way and I came up with the idea of Little Leyla. Insha'Allah Leyla can help inspire even the youngest ones to incorporate Allah in all things they do throughout the day in a fun and easy way.

www.ingramcontent.com/pod-product-compliance
Lightning Source LLC
LaVergne TN
LVHW010316070426
835510LV00024B/3408